OMNIBUS PRESS PRESENTS THE STORY OF
GOOD CHARLOTTE

Exclusive Distributors:
Music Sales Limited,
8/9 Frith Street, London W1D 3JB, UK

Music Sales Corporation,
257 Park Avenue South, New York, NY 10010, USA

Macmillan Distribution Services,
53 Park West Drive, Derrimut, Vic 3030, Australia

To the Music Trade only:
Music Sales Limited
8/9 Frith Street, London W1D 3JB, UK

Photo Credits:
Front cover: Hayley Madden/Retna
Back cover: John Spellman/Retna
Daniel Coston/Retna (1, 40, 43 & 85), Amanda Edwards/LFI (2 & 79), George Campos/LFI (4),
Carmen Valdes/Retna (7), Matt Smith/Getty Images (8 & 17), Michael Williams/LFI (10 & 75),
Frank White (13, 30, 50, 55 & 95), Kelly Swift (14 & 34), Daniel Berehulak/Getty Images (18),
Jan Goedefroit/LFI (19), Max Franklin/Getty Images (20), Kellie Warren/Getty Images (22),
Frank Micelotta/Getty Images (23, 25, 72 & 80), Steve Double/Retna (24),
John E. Ksako/Retna (27 & 56), Marc Larkin/LFI (28), Jeff Kroll/LFI (31), Jen Lowery (32),
Evan Agostini/Getty Images (35b), Yael/Retna (35t), Scott Harrison/Getty Images (36),
Justin Borucki/Retna (38b), Larry Marano/LFI (38t, 39, 92), BJ Papas/Retna (42, 44 & 70),
Kevin Parry/LFI (45), Steve Sands/Corbis (47), Win Mcnamee/Corbis (49), Awais Butt/LFI (52),
Zach Cordner/Retna (54), Scott Weiner/Retna (58), Scott Gries/Getty Images (59, 62 & 82),
David Atlas/Retna (65 & 76), Paul Smith/Retna (66), Jon James/LFI (67),
Dennis Van Tine/LFI (86), Stefan Zaklin/Corbis (88), Joseph Marzullo/Retna (91)

Printed in the USA
by Vicks Lithograph and Printing Corp.

Visit Omnibus Press at www.omnibuspress.com

OMNIBUS PRESS PRESENTS THE STORY OF

GOOD CHARLOTTE

DOUG SMALL

OMNIBUS PRESS
LONDON · NEW YORK · SYDNEY

AN irresistible mix of punk, pop, and rock, Good Charlotte's music defies definition yet appeals to the mainstream. Well-crafted songs that pack a punch with their personal, honest lyrics have secured the band an intensely devoted fan base. Nearly constant touring has earned them a reputation as one of the hardest working lineups out there, and the group's infectious love of performance has made them one of today's must-see live acts.

Good Charlotte is a study in contradictions. Headed by identical twins who don't look alike, inspired by hardcore street punk and Frank Sinatra, this is a band that has managed to hold on tight to its rock credentials while topping the TRL charts. Covered in tattoos and body piercings and with a fondness for multicolored hair fashioned into six-inch spikes, these are some of the most down-to-earth guys you'll ever want to meet.

Who would have thought that a bunch of small-town high school misfits could conquer the pop music world through sheer determination? Here's their story. . . .

COMPLICATED

DENTICAL twins Benji and Joel were born on March 11, 1979, five minutes apart. They grew up in Waldorf, Maryland, located in Charles County, just twenty-three miles south of Washington, D.C. Considered part of the D.C. metro area, it is, in other words, "the middle-of-nowhere suburbs," as Benji puts it in the Good Charlotte website bio.

The twins looked very much alike in their early pre-tattoo days, but Benji was branded early on as the troublemaker. Whenever one of the adorable little boys misbehaved, Benji was automatically to blame, and he took a lot of punishment rightfully belonging to the angelic Joel. The twins pulled the irresistible trick of impersonating one another at school and would even attend each other's classes. When they were younger it was easy to pull off; their parents couldn't resist dressing them alike up until the fifth grade when they rebelled and started developing their own style. Benji even went so far as to pretend to be his brother in order to help him out with the opposite sex, calling girls on the phone on his shyer sibling's behalf.

It was the close relationship between the twins that formed the foundation for Good Charlotte. Even today, when the band is its own incredibly close-knit family unit, there is still an even stronger bond between the two brothers. Guitar player Billy Martin admits on *The Young and the Hopeless* CD Extra that it can be difficult to contend with at times, saying,

"SOMETIMES IT'S FRUSTRATING BECAUSE THEY HAVE THEIR OWN LITTLE WORLD. YOU KNOW, IT'S LIKE THEY HAVE THIS COMMUNICATION THAT NOBODY ELSE CAN REALLY HAVE OR UNDERSTAND."

Bassist Paul Thomas recognizes the twins' unique connection, saying, "It seems like they can read each other's thoughts sometimes." Benji and Joel themselves are the first to admit that the way that they are interconnected is above and beyond any other relationship they have crafted in life. And it was this tenable link that would see them through some very hard times.

In 1995, midway through their high school careers, the twins managed to get a couple of the last tickets going for a concert on a Beastie Boys tour at the Patriot Center. Virtually last-row seats notwithstanding, Benji and Joel were blown away. Fans of the band since grade school—when Benji turned up on "Rock Star Day" dressed as Mike D—the brothers emerged from the show with one thought in mind: This was what they wanted to do. Their determination was not hampered one bit by a distinct lack of musical prowess. They began attending every show that came to town, and were further inspired by the live acts of Rage Against the Machine, Silverchair, and Rancid.

Despite their mother's preference for religious music, the brothers managed to develop a covert fondness for pop, rock, alternative, punk—you name it. As Joel would years later recant to *Rolling Stone* in its November 21, 2002, issue, "My mom is a Christian, and she wouldn't let us listen to rock music. So me and my brother, we had this tape player with headphones, and we locked ourselves in our pantry. We were fighting over the headphones, sitting in this dark pantry listening to Metallica." Discovering Nirvana was a major moment. The twins raided their older brother Josh's record collection which featured the Cure, the Dead Milkmen, Rancid, and the Smiths, and started rushing home from school to work on writing songs together. Benji picked up an old guitar that had been hanging around the house gathering dust and taught himself to play with a little help from La Plata High band director Timothy Bodamer; Joel, with the Smiths' lead singer Morrissey as a role model, took over the vocal side of the burgeoning musical partnership.

Benji and Joel may have been spending a lot of time locked away listening to music, but they were far from unaware of the tension between their parents. Their father, reportedly an alcoholic, was volatile and unpredictable. "If he came home and his shoes weren't in the right place," Joel told *Rolling Stone* in its May 1, 2003, issue, "he would just start going off. One time I saw him rip a phone, like, in one motion, rip the phone off the wall and throw it at my mom—like he was pitching a baseball." On Christmas Eve 1995 there was another argument, and the twins' father stormed out. This in itself wasn't remarkable, although his timing wasn't particularly festive. Then the unimaginable happened: He never came back. Ever.

Without the main breadwinner's income—the twins' father had heretofore supported his wife and four children through employment as a butcher as well as with house-painting jobs—the family found themselves in dire financial trouble. The bank foreclosed on their house. Benji and Joel were abruptly ousted from a home on a wooded lot which had afforded them their own separate bedrooms for the first time in their lives. The family was homeless. The sense of disorientation when suddenly faced with the void their father had left behind was only compounded by the loss of their home. Local relatives offered temporary refuge, but crowding in to already full households was far from ideal. The family finally found a place to stay in the form of a vacant farmhouse which a kindhearted farmer offered for their use. The twins' mom began supporting the family through receptionist and hairstylist jobs.

Just when things were pretty bad, they got worse. The twins' mother was diagnosed with lupus, and was put in a hospital. Benji and Joel now felt responsible for keeping the family afloat. They picked up whatever work they could find—mainly at a revolving roster of local area restaurants—and even took on a brief joint stint sudsing up the customers as shampooers at a hair salon. While other kids their age were moonlighting at odd jobs to earn cash to take to the mall, for Benji and Joel, this was serious business. The pressing burden of paying household bills in order to keep the lights on, the phone connected, and the car running can be stressful enough for an adult, much less a teenager. They would often go for days at a time without heat, as they just didn't have the money to buy oil.

"When my dad left, I was always the one that was kind of, like, crying about it, like, 'Why us, why us?' Lucky for me, I had Benj," Joel recalled to *Rolling Stone* magazine in its May 1, 2003, issue. "We've always been sidekicks. The chip he had on his shoulder was more out of necessity back then. But we always had each other all the time to say,

'MAN, DON'T WORRY. IT'LL BE ALL RIGHT, IT'LL GET BETTER.'"

REARRANGING

BENJI and Joel turned to their newfound love of music with even more fervor in the midst of such tumultuous home circumstances. Music became their haven, often the one and only positive aspect of their day-to-day lives, and it took on tremendous importance to the two brothers.

They soon recruited friends and fellow La Plata High students Paul Thomas, a bassist, and Aaron Escolopio, a drummer, to expand their musical endeavor. Now they had a proper lineup. Paul, born October 5, 1980, was the son of a Waldorf police officer father. An overweight theater geek with a penchant for cardigans and

white socks, he gave up the lead in the school play to dedicate himself to the fledgling band. Naming themselves Good Charlotte after the children's book by Carol Beach York, the boys were ready to rock. Well, sort of. Their first live performance—in the hot and happening venue of a neighbor's basement in front of a few dozen pals—may not have been up to Warped standards, but the band did play a full set of songs they'd penned themselves. This was no wedding band! Truth be told, the brothers were so busy writing their own music they hadn't had a chance to learn anyone else's. "We had our first band practice maybe two weeks after I started playing guitar," Benji recalled to

Hip Online on October 16, 2000. "I knew three chords: D, G, and A! I became fascinated with all of the late-Seventies punks. There was something about those old recordings, those seven-inch singles. . . . There's no music that sounds like that today because of the raw quality."

Rawness was certainly one quality the beginning band could lay claim to, but they stuck with it, although they were still very much the novices—and it showed. During their early performances, Joel was sometimes so overcome with discomfiture that he would turn his back to the audience and sing to the wall. Benji described the first "concert" to *Livewire* on November 16, 2001, saying, "There was only like thirty kids there, but we were really nervous, and my face, like, I wasn't used to getting up in front

of people really. . . . I was just looking down the whole time and we messed up like every song. And I still have the set list. But you know, I look back now, it was funny and I laugh. It was cool. We were such little kids, you know?"

The Good Charlotte guys weren't disheartened by their beginner's glitches, nor were they put off by a deficit of hot record industry contacts. In keeping with the punk edict, they got on with it themselves. Benji remembers the brothers' naïve optimism in their official website bio, saying, "I wrote this letter saying, 'We're Good Charlotte and if you sign us now it will be a lot cheaper than if you wait!' Our ignorance was kind of a blessing. We couldn't be discouraged by knowing too much about how the business really works." Their homegrown publicity kits included a bio and a press photo taken by none other than the twins' little sister, Sarah. Benji and Joel knew they had a lot to learn, and the band took top priority. The days of hanging out at Ledo's pizzeria and the St. Charles Town Center shopping mall would soon be a thing of the past—they had places to go, and they needed a lot of practice!

"We really weren't that good," Joel openly admitted in *Billboard's* November 4, 2000, edition.

"BUT WE JUST GAVE OUR WHOLE LIVES TO IT. WE PRACTICED ALL THE TIME, AND BENJI AND I WROTE ALL THE TIME. OUR WHOLE ATTITUDE IS POSITIVITY. WE DON'T HAVE ANY HIGHER GOALS."

Tough as things were at home, high school was no picnic. Torment took many forms, from run-of-the-mill verbal tauntings to more inventive varieties of teenage torture. There was, for instance, the reported Bengay incident when Joel was secured to a bench in the boys' locker room and generously slathered with the mentholated substance in a spot where the sun doesn't shine. Paul, meanwhile, was temporarily expelled for allegedly threatening the principal with a punch in the face. As soon as the guys' musical aspirations became known, the prank calls started with a vengeance: classmates posing as record label executives relentlessly telephoned the twins' house offering them big label deals.

The twins resisted the seriously contemplated temptation to drop out of school—they just couldn't do that to their mom—although Joel admits to having failed a social studies class geared entirely toward preparation for college. He had no intention of getting a university degree; his sole goal was to make a success of Good Charlotte. As he later told VH-1 in an online interview on April 4, 2003, "We were doing this whole semester of career things. We had to take these aptitude tests. You had to fill out all these questions and then there's a whole list of careers to choose. I was looking at it and thought, 'I don't want to be any of these jobs! I want to do music.' The teachers were like, 'Well, music's not a real job.' I refused to do the test. It was like an eight-week college prep course and I failed the class because they didn't have any options I wanted to do. In a small town like the one where I came from, nobody believed that music could be a real job."

MOTIVATE ME

BENJI and Joel graduated in 1997, and made the definite decision to forego a college education in order to pursue their musical aspirations. Presented with two airline tickets to California as a graduation gift from their mother, the twins hopped on a plane for the first time in their lives and made a pilgrimage to a punk rock shrine: 924 Gilman Street, the club that had spawned the first major success story of the new generation of pop punksters in Green Day. After checking out the West Coast scene, Joel and Benji returned home duly motivated and ready to rumble.

They packed up and moved to Annapolis, where there was a much more extensive range of gigging opportunities. The band paid its dues and polished its chops in front of crowds all over the city, playing anywhere that would book them. The greenhorn group knew that the only way to get a professional live act together was to play, play, play—and stay positive in the face of adversity. They fully realized that they needed a lot of work, and they were willing to put in the time. "There were so many shitty shows," Benji reminisced to *Rolling Stone* in its September 27, 2002, edition. "There was this one show we played, and the bar owner actually tried to make us pay him." More established local bands helped break the young band in; the members of Jimmie's Chicken Shack were kind and supportive enough to lob coasters at the Good Charlotte guys during their gigs to toughen them up a bit. All in good fun, of course.

Newest and youngest band member Billy Martin (born June 15, 1981) soon brought another guitar to the mix. Billy turned up at one of the twins' acoustic gigs and liked what he heard. He became friendly with the two brothers, and when they were evicted from their apartment they moved into his house. "They said—we need to find a new apartment, can we crash at

your place for two weeks? And I said of course you can," Billy recalled in an October 8, 2002, BBC Radio 1 interview. "Ten months later they were talking about probably moving out soon. Pretty funny." Billy was still a high school student, although his shoulder-length dreadlocks and affinity for wearing makeup to school didn't exactly help him fit in. He felt more comfortable in the company of the older twins, and once he discovered that they shared his admiration for Australian band Silverchair, it was a done deal. He left his own band, Overflow, and became a bona fide member of Good Charlotte. Billy, whose other musical influences included the Deftones, Incubus, and Korn, was inspired to pursue a musical career after coming across Silverchair when he was fourteen years of age and working at McDonald's. The Aussie rockers were only fifteen and had already released a record, and Billy was determined to follow in their footsteps.

Silverchair

Needless to say, Good Charlotte's music wasn't (yet) paying the rent. The twins picked up whatever work they could find: "all kinds of shitty jobs—I've had over thirty of them," Benji says on the band's website.

"IT WAS A STRUGGLING TIME IN OUR LIVES, BUT IT WAS ALSO A GREAT TIME. IT'S GOOD TO BE HUNGRY SOMETIMES."

The future rock stars waited tables at various local restaurants, painted houses, washed cars, and worked at the likes of American Eagle Outfitters, Borders Bookstore, Food Lion Supermarket, and Target. Playing gigs late at night often interfered with that early-morning wakeup call for work the next day, and most jobs lasted only a few months. Benji's Target gig actually ended on an unusually bad note. He was relegated to unpacking trucks out the back of the store as his multicolored hair and fondness for tattoos didn't quite conform to the dress code, and one day he snuck into a company picnic without contributing the requested $5 fee and then proceeded to yell at a woman who confronted him. She turned out to be his manager's wife, and that was the end of that. A bit of luck came along however when Benji's next job as a waiter at an Annapolis eatery and club, the Acme Bar & Grill, translated into a regular gig for Good Charlotte.

An unflagging positive attitude was what kept the guys going. They were determined that things would get better, and they were dedicated to their music. "It was the hardest of times," Benji told *Entertainment Weekly* in the magazine's October 30, 2002, edition. "But our band got us through. It was what we dreamed about." Joel recalled to *MTV News* on April 13, 2001, how he would ask himself, "'Am I ever gonna get to where I won't have to wonder if I'm going to get kicked out of the place I'm staying? If I'm gonna be able to eat tomorrow? Is our band ever going to get signed? Is this ever going to happen?' You just want to get out of it, you want to get out of the rut you're stuck in." Being dead broke is no fun, and both brothers considered packing it all in for a more conventional lifestyle that would afford them somewhere to live and a few creature comforts, but they continued to motivate each other and stuck with their dream.

THE CLICK

SLOWLY but surely the band's resolve began to pay off. Staff members of Washington, D.C., radio station WHFS were impressed with Good Charlotte's chops at a bar gig and began playing the band's music on the air in the form of a "Little Things" demo. "Can't Go On" was featured on a music sampler after the band won a local contest. Philadelphia station WPLY soon followed suit with Good Charlotte airplay after the band played its first big show as support for the punk/ska outfit Save Ferris.

Then a 1999 support slot with Lit on a sold-out East Coast tour presented the band with an amazing opportunity. "We had no money, no transportation, and no way to do the gigs. Our mom was living in like a shed on a neighbor's property, and the only thing she really owned was a minivan. She said, 'You guys take the minivan to play the shows and I'll catch rides or walk to work.' That just shows you how she's been there for us the whole time," Benji says in the official website bio. Mom's support for the band's first long-term tour would soon lead to a grueling future schedule of over 300 shows each year.

Legend has it that one of those unsolicited demo tapes mailed out with naïve optimism incredibly hit its mark when in 1999 a mailroom clerk brought a Good Charlotte cassette to the attention of Sony's mid-Atlantic promotion manager Mike Martinovich. Representatives from several major labels were amongst the crowd at the December 1999 New York City gig with Lit. The band didn't let their nerves show, although Benji later admitted to being so blown away by the sheer size of New York City that he just wanted to go home. Home was not an option, however; this was a concert in front of an audience peppered with record company A&R guys who wielded the power to grant Good Charlotte its ultimate wish. The band gave it their all, and unbeknownst to them they would soon see the fruit of their punked-up labor.

Meanwhile, the days of one-off local gigs had morphed into full-time supporting touring spots. The band honed their skills and learned the ropes on the road in 2000, playing with the likes of Lit, Eve 6, and Goldfinger. They played to small crowds in intimate clubs during a tour with Sum 41 and Mest. Each and every show was another chance for the GC crew to develop their stage presence and to learn how to connect with their audience. In fact, the Good Charlotte guys were still known to actually join the audience during the other bands' sets, and even crowd-surfed their way through an Eve 6 performance one evening. Just because they were in a

band themselves didn't mean that they weren't still fans as well.

Although their touring schedule was very full, the band made sure to put aside some time for charitable work. "We plan on starting to visit hospitals while we are on tour," Benji revealed during a September 25, 2000, Lycos online chat. "And we're involved with a clothing company called East Coast Clothing and in conjunction with that we're going to be visiting sick children and try to bring joy to their lives." The band played

at any charity-related functions they heard about, including benefits for the Annapolis Rape Center and the Leukemia Foundation. Charity work was important to Good Charlotte from day one, and would remain a priority in the years to come.

D.C. radio station WHFS continued to have a hand in getting the Good Charlotte word out. On February 25, 2000, Benji, Joel, and the guys played the HFS-kimo Snow Job festival along with Lit, Long Beach Dub Allstars, and the Suicide Machines. In May, the band found themselves at another WHFS Spring HFStival, this time exposing them to an even broader audience as they shared the main stage with headliners Stone Temple Pilots, Cypress Hill, Rage against the Machine, and Third Eye Blind at the sold-out event. As WHFS Program Director Robert Benjamin said in the November 12, 2000, edition of the *Washington Post*, "Benji once told me they wanted to be a combination of the Backstreet Boys and Minor Threat. They want to be big, they want to be famous, but they also have real punk-rock roots, and that's really important." Big and famous they were soon to be, mainly owing to the nonstop touring that garnered the band an ever-growing fan base.

And then it happened. In May 2000, Good Charlotte found themselves gripping that much-coveted, rarely obtained music industry brass ring: a record deal. David Massey, Epic Record's Executive Vice President of A&R, called the signing "a no-brainer." The guys of Good Charlotte could hardly believe that what they had been striving for and dreaming about had actually come true.

The ever-churning machine that is the music industry began to take notice. The music biz bible, *Billboard*, featured the little-known upstarts in its "Popular Uprisings" section on September 16, 2000, noting that "Annapolis, Md.–based modern rock band Good Charlotte is off to a promising start."

Daylight/Epic Records' newest debut, *Good Charlotte*, was released on September 26, and although reviews were lukewarm ("This is all standard-issue stuff"—*All Music Guide*), and sales were nothing to write home about, the band was up and running, and destined to succeed. The album was primarily recorded in Los Angeles' Encore Studios, and was produced by Don Gilmore, who had previously worked with Eve 6 and Lit. "What drew me to the band the most was their personality," he said to *Hip Online* on October 16, 2000. "There's a lot of pop-punk rock bands that have gotten record deals, but these guys are doing something really different."

THE LITTLE THINGS

"**L**ITTLE THINGS" was the hit single out of the gate. The song struck a chord with so many high-school-aged kids who, after one listen, were dedicated disciples of their new favorite band, Good Charlotte. Aside from its fresh, catchy sound, the song's lyrics captured common adolescent angst (*Like the time in school when we got free lunch, and the cool kids beat us up / And the rich kids had convertibles, and we had to ride the bus*) as well as touching upon the twins' deeply personal anguish describing their mother's breakdown and their father's sudden departure (*And that same year on Christmas Eve, Dad went to the store / We checked his room, his things were gone, we didn't see him no more*). The downtrodden youth of the nation was gratified to discover an empathetic voice, and were impressed with such a refreshingly honest take on pop music. "Everything we say is straight from our hearts," Joel told the *Washington Times* on February 15, 2001.

"WE CAN'T WRITE A FAKE SONG. EVERYTHING WE WRITE IS EITHER SELF-CONFESSIONAL OR BASED ON A TRUE STORY. EVERYONE IS GOING TO KNOW EVERYTHING ABOUT MY LIFE THREE ALBUMS INTO THIS."

He went on to explain, "A lot of our fans have gone through some of the things our music talks about. So to hear someone else express what they feel really means a lot to them."

The album's songs brought to the forefront the personal difficulties Benji and Joel had been through while generating a universal message of hope. The prevailing notion that "Everything will be alright"—a recurring lyric—caused fans to write to the twins to tell them that Good Charlotte's music was the only thing getting them through some tough times. Kids missing a dad felt that they had a real connection with the band. Girl

troubles, school troubles, home troubles. . .these were all laid out in the open on the album, and young fans felt an extraordinary devotion to the band. "We want to give kids something to hope for," Benji told *Teen People* in its May 12, 2003, issue.

"IF ONE KID SAYS, 'YOUR CD HELPED GET ME THROUGH THIS YEAR,' THAT'S ALL IT TAKES."

The "Little Things" video takes us all back to those tortuous teenage days—albeit to the fictional Waldorf High where the snotty hottie is played by none other than Mandy Moore. When asked how they had managed to

get the hot pop star to appear in the clip during a *TV Guide* online chat on September 21, 2000, Benji replied, "I waited outside of [her] house for three weeks. No. . . . She's on our record label so we knew some people that worked with her and we had people between us. The idea came up, we called her and she said 'Yes' and I stuttered."

The video is a feel-good revenge fantasy for every geek and freak who's ever attended high school. Joel kick-starts the payback by bursting into the principal's office and commandeering the P.A. system to address the student body. His dedications ("This is for is every kid who's ever been picked last in gym class, to every kid who's never had a date to no school dance, to everyone who's ever been called a freak!") are met with a huge grin from the class nerd and a lip-curled nod of approval from a tattooed punk. Delighted kids sitting in the classroom begin to rock along—this beats the pledge of allegiance hands-down. The Good Charlotte guys then take a tour of the school grounds, confronting the jocks and cheerleaders and cool rich kids who alternately snubbed and abused them and generally made their high school careers a complete misery. In the end, punk triumphs over popular and the band takes over the school auditorium for an impromptu concert. Even the principal's sour-faced attempt to put a stop to the festivities is preempted by a heroic janitor, and at the end of the video we all feel like cheering. The clip was a real breakthrough for Good Charlotte, proving itself very popular on MTV; high rotation on that station is priceless for any hopeful up-and-coming band.

The second single, "Motivation Proclamation," was a tune destined to inspire and encourage every lazy layabout out there to get up and do something with their lives. The driving, rocking chorus says it all: *Motivate me, I wanna get myself out of this bed / Captivate me, I want good thoughts inside of my head*. The video portrays the band members moping around the house, watching cartoons, drinking milk straight out the bottle, and generally feeling sorry for themselves in true couch-potato style. Once the band starts to rock out in the middle of the living room, Joel jumps up from the front porch where he has been moodily staring out into the distance and grabs the mike to join in.

Another standout track on the album is "Festival Song," a tribute of sorts to WHFS and its HFStival. The track's video brings us all into the daytime summer festival performance world, and captures the live Good Charlotte experience to a T. Also noteworthy is the extremely touching hidden track "Thank You Mom." Benji and Joel chose not to use their father's last name on the album credits or indeed in any publicity or press, and the other band members followed suit out of courtesy and understanding. In later years, Benji and Joel adopted their mother's maiden name, Madden, and the others re-tacked their own surnames back in place. The band also later redesigned the *Good Charlotte* album cover.

It takes just one look at the album's "thank you" section of the liner notes to realize that the band members have very strongly held religious beliefs and that their faith is of utmost importance to them. Benji (who, by the way, sports a tattoo of the Virgin Mary on his neck) thanks "my lord and savior Jesus Christ for giving me all of these opportunities." Joel is straight out of the gate with, "First I would like to thank my heavenly Father, and Lord and Savior Jesus Christ who is always faithful even when I am not. Thank you Lord for your understanding and patience." Aaron, Billy, and Paul all give God a shout-out as well. Benji matter-of-factly explains the band's attitude toward religion to the *Washington Times* in its May 2, 2003, edition, saying, "Our spirituality is just part of [our] lives. We are who we are, and if it makes us more punk or less punk, we don't care." He goes on to address the fans, stating, "We are four kids from Waldorf. We're no better than any other band out there, and we know it. Thanks for giving us a chance to do what we love."

The album was not a huge chart-topping hit, but it was a major label album, and to the GC guys, that was what mattered. All in all, *Good Charlotte* was an impressive introduction to the songwriting capabilities of the two brothers. Joel and Benji's harmonies lent a distinctive edge to the music, but it was truly the subject matter that elevated this debut album above those of its pop-rock-punk cohorts.

BAND OF BROTHERS

THE musical partnership between the brothers certainly benefits from their twinly tendencies. A songwriting team since day one, Benji and Joel had morphed into a formidable creative force fueled by a singularity of vision not often found in the music business. Most songwriting teams have experienced the angst that is borne of disparate ideas—hence the term "creative differences" that is so often used to explain away the dissolution of many a great band—but the Madden twins operate with a one-mindedness that has proven extremely fruitful. Their joint venture is all the more successful due to a refreshing lack of ego. The twins are never competitive; they are supportive of each other to a fault, and this mutual backup system works like a charm.

Despite their personal and musical bond, the twins are distinctly different in many ways. Benji sees himself as the leader—"self-proclaimed leader" he cheerfully admits —of the band, and he is a bit protective of Joel. "Joel's kind of—not dependant—but he's definitely kind of innocent," Benji reveals on the *The Young and the Hopeless* CD Extra. "I'm kind of the older brother . . . sometimes I act like it, sometimes I don't!"

The twins, surprisingly, don't share musical tastes. Joel's idols include Morrissey and Frank Sinatra, while Benji has been known to lean more towards street punk. Joel seems to be the romantic, confessing to spending a lot of quality time as a teenager listening to the Cure and reveling in his heartbroken status over this or that girl. Benji, meanwhile, was busy guarding that chip on his shoulder. Their personal senses of style are also quite dissimilar. Benji goes for the extreme. His ever-changing hairstyle has included six-inch Liberty spikes, leopard spots, and a rainbow of colors. Joel meanwhile favors plain old black, and while he may sport the odd Mohawk-inspired do, usually opts for a fairly conservative look. Both

brothers have a fondness for tattoos—the first tattoo they both got is an Irish flag to represent their Irish roots—but it's Benji who has gone the whole hog with regard to body art and piercings.

"I think Benj is a little bit more outgoing and in your face," Joel told *Music Head* on December 29, 2000. "I'm a little bit more reserved and quiet and conservative in some ways. Benj is wild, you never know what to expect out of him. He's out of control sometimes, and that's the way he is and I love him for it. I wouldn't change one thing about him. We're just like Ying and Yang, me and him, like night and day sometimes. He's really outspoken and he says what he thinks right away."

Despite Joel's less outgoing nature, he comes into his own when it comes to performing onstage. "Joel's got this flair, this spark—that's why he's the lead singer—and a lot of times he can take a song from being just okay to being great," Benji explained on the Sony Music Australia website on July 18, 2003. "At other times, he'll have ideas and not know what to do with them. But I'm good with structures and arrangements, so we work well together even though we're really different people."

TRUE to the band's work ethic, they didn't sit back and wait for the world to notice Epic's newest sound. They took to the road with an even stronger sense of purpose. The van became their home away from home, but aside from little arguments from time to time, they took to life on the road like punk ducks to water. The five guys from Waldorf were getting to see the entire country, gig by gig. Sure, they relied on PlayStation for a bit of entertainment now and then, but all in all they truly enjoyed every aspect of touring. "You get really used to living out of the bag and to meeting new people every day and being in new situations, new surroundings every day," Joel told *Music Head* in a December 29, 2000, interview. "I don't think any band has the right to complain because I think we're so lucky to be able to do this and be on the road and play every day and meet people. I mean when I hear a lot of rock and pop stars

GET A REAL JOB

and pop stars complaining, it makes me sick. Because I'm like, this is a dream come true, you know, it's amazing."

Getting to know fellow musicians from all over the country was an incredible experience for the Waldorf crew. An October 5, 2000, gig at one of their favorite old haunts, the 9:30 Club in Washington, D.C., saw Good Charlotte sharing the bill with Houston, Texas, group Fenix*TX, Southern California rock quartet Lefty, and most notably a band that would become great friends and co-headliners: Florida punk outfit New Found Glory.

The GC crew kept the momentum going, rounding out 2000 with a three-month-long stint touring with MxPx, the Washington State Christian punk band. A real highlight was a homecoming gig on New Year's Eve with old friends Jimmie's Chicken Shack and Jepetto. By the end of the year they had made great strides toward establishing the high-energy live show that they are known for today.

The beginning of the New Year found the guys back in high school, but this time instead of being greeted with bullying and insults they were hailed

NEW FOUND GLORY

by a cheering crowd when they hit the stage in the Arundel High School gym. The students had won their very own Good Charlotte concert in a canned-food drive contest sponsored by WHFS, and it was yet another charity-linked event for the band.

Good Charlotte then took part in what would prove to be the first of many

collaborations with MTV when in November they recorded the theme music for a new animated series called "Undergrads" which was slated to air in spring 2001. The show would also feature Good Charlotte cartoon characters.

That spring, Good Charlotte played the New Jersey Skate and Surf Festival along with New Found Glory, the Descendents, and the Get Up Kids. They then hit the road with MxPx once again, this time co-supporting along with Californian pop-punk group Slick Shoes, playing gigs throughout March, April, and May in California, Canada, Colorado, Connecticut, Florida, Georgia, Illinois, Indiana, Kansas, Michigan, Minnesota, Missouri, Nevada, New Jersey, New York, North Carolina, Ohio, Oklahoma, Pennsylvania, South Carolina, Tennessee, Texas, Utah, Washington, and Wisconsin, and yet another spot at the good old 9:30 Club in Washington, D.C. Toward the end of the tour the practical jokes began to fly, and during one show the GC guys brought a table and chairs out on stage and had

Beastie Boys Mike D

themselves some dinner right in the middle of MxPx's set! Then came Memorial Day weekend, and how better to celebrate the beginning of summer than at the WHFStival? This year's gala was held at the RFK Stadium and featured Benji's first hero, the Beastie Boys' Mike D, as well as Coldplay, Fatboy Slim, Linkin Park, Live, Staind, Three Doors Down, and many others.

The nearly constant touring schedule they had set for themselves was earning Good Charlotte an ever-growing reputation as a kicking live act, and kids really took to the band that wasn't above hanging with the fans. "Meeting fans is awesome and kids that are really into the music, that's what we've always wanted." Billy told *Ear Candy* on April 22, 2001.

"SO IT'S A GOOD FEELING WHEN KIDS GET EXCITED AND LIKE TO COME TO THE SHOWS. WE SPEND A MAJORITY OF THE SHOW AFTER THE PLAYING JUST WALKING AROUND THE CROWD AND MEETING KIDS. KIDS ARE LIKE 'WHY DO YOU DO THIS?' AND WE SAY, 'WELL IF IT WASN'T FOR YOU GUYS WE WOULD BE NOTHING.' IT'S LIKE IT MAKES SENSE TO US JUST TO HANG OUT 'CAUSE WE LIKE TO."

The time they spent chatting with kids from big cities and small towns, hanging out and finding out what their fans were up to and into was all a part of the touring experience to the GC guys.

WARPED SPEED AHEAD

GOOD CHARLOTTE's touring status was about to take a step up the punk-rock ladder. The band had landed a very desirable slot on the 2001 Warped Tour. Warped, a traveling circus of music, sports, and all things punk was an ingenious vehicle for introducing like-minded music fans to a spectrum of bands. Featuring both established headlining groups and artists as well as lesser-known bands on the rise, all performing throughout the day and into the evening on a network of different stages, Warped gave its audience a day to remember. The 2001 tour was to bring in over 450,000 fans and a $6 million profit—and everybody wins. The young concertgoers win with an affordable average ticket price of $25 and get real bang for the buck with more music and activity than they can swallow in one day. The bands win, as they get exposure to a huge potential fan base, most of whom may not have heard of them prior to the festival but who go home newly converted followers.

Just as they were preparing themselves for the Warped experience, Aaron left the band. Good Charlotte hastened to make it clear that there were absolutely no hard feelings, posting the news on their website, saying, "Hello everyone, it's Benji, Paul, Joel, and Billy. We have some news for you that we wanted to tell all of you ourselves. . . . Aaron has left Good Charlotte to pursue his own band effort. All five of us talked about this and made a mutual decision. As supporters of Good Charlotte, we hope you understand and respect everyone's feelings on this. We wish Aaron well." Aaron went on to join his brother Ryan in the band Wakefield, and had this to say: "The hard part was leaving four guys that's been a part of my life for the past six years. Good Charlotte has been good to me, I'll miss those guys a lot and wish them the best. Sometimes you have to do things that don't make sense when your heart tells you to, and this was just one of those times."

The timing wasn't exactly key, however; they urgently had to find a replacement drummer to take with them on tour. Luckily, they found a good fit in Dusty, a drummer who had previously played with Washington, D.C., bands Jesus Eater and the Misery. "We're from the same scene, and he was hanging out in the same circles of people that we were hanging out with." Joel told *Philly Underground* in an October 21, 2001, interview. "We had two days to find a drummer for Warped Tour, and Dusty said he'd come over, so we gave him our CD, and the next day, we went over there and played with him. He's a great drummer, but his attitude at first was just so great; he's such a good guy, and he just wants to play music. That's what we wanted to find because that's what we needed in our band—we needed someone who was more like us." Dusty, however, would not ultimately stay the course.

The Warped Tour kicked off on June 22 in the blazing heat of Peoria, Arizona. Despite the 110-degree temperature, the crowd turned up in droves at the Peoria Sports Complex. Rancid took the stage during the slightly cooler evening hours, but New Found Glory performed during peak sunshine, and lead singer Jordan Pundik shouted out the academic question,

"WHO HERE'S HOT?"

New Found Glory's Jordan Pundik

The lineup was definitely hot, also featuring Alien Ant Farm, Assjack, Fear, H20, Less than Jake, Detroit rappers Natas, and 311. Highlights included Me First and the Gimme Gimmes treating the young crowd to their punk cover versions of decidedly non-punk classics like "Take Me Home, Country Roads," and "Over the Rainbow." Hank III (rebellious son of country legend Hank Williams, Jr.) stood out on one of the six stages with his unorthodox take on punk rock featuring a fiddler and a stand-up bass. Good Charlotte's first Warped set didn't start out auspiciously; a sound problem hampered the first song and Joel's vocals were nonexistent, but the guys persevered and the crowd gave them an enthusiastic reception.

Other bands on the tour included AFI, the Ataris, Big Wig, the Distillers, Dub Pistols, Esham, Fenix*TX, Grand Theft Auto, Guttermouth, Jepetto, the Juliana Theory, Kill Your Idols, Kool Keith, Madcap, Midtown, the Misfits, Morgan Heritage, No Motiv, Pennywise, River City Rebels, Rollins Band, Saves the Day, Sugarcult, the Vandals, Userfriendly, and Weezer. Another unconventional group to hit the stage was Incredibly Strange Wrestling, a, well, incredibly strange punk/wrestling fusion formed in San Francisco and boasting hardcore wrestlers El Homo Loco and Macho Sasquatcho.

Playing alongside the very same bands they had idolized and listened to throughout their teen years was thrilling and often daunting for the GC crew. When Rancid, one of Benji and Joel's favorite bands, dubbed Good Charlotte Rancid's "little brothers" the guys were in rock credibility heaven. The two bands got so close that Rancid's Lars was kind enough to lend his skills and give Benji a tattoo that summer.

ME FIRST AND THE GIMME GIMMES

The Warped Tour rocketed along virtually nonstop with forty-three dates through the summer, making its warped way along the West Coast, through Middle America, and on to the East Coast, touching down in most major cities including Atlanta, Boston, Dallas, Las Vegas, Los Angeles, Miami, Nashville, New York City, Pittsburgh, Salt Lake City, and San Francisco, winding down to the final gig on August 12, in Pontiac, Michigan. Warped, known to insiders as Punk Rock Summer Camp, had definitely taught Good Charlotte a thing or two.

I DON'T WANNA STOP

THE GC guys kept the momentum going as they joined up with yet another tour, this time supporting one of their favorite bands, Blink-182, along with Jimmy Eat World, New Found Glory, and Sum 41. The bands made it all the way to Canada for the Edgefest II.

In the wake of the terrorist attacks on the United States, Good Charlotte recorded a 9/11 tribute song called "The Innocent" with Goldfinger's John Feldman and Mest. All proceeds went to the Red Cross and other organizations set up to help the victims and their families.

Good Charlotte wrapped up the Blink tour and headed much further afield, braving the seemingly endless plane ride to Australia in October. It was the full band's first trip to Australia, although Benji and Joel had been once before on a short acoustic tour. Playing Down Under at the Livid Festival in Brisbane along with their friends H20 and lots of top Aussie bands was quite an experience. Good Charlotte also performed a series of their own gigs which were well attended due to the popularity of "Little Things," a huge radio hit in the Land of Oz. Their October 10 gig at Sydney's Bar Broadway was a sold-out show full of pogoing Aussies singing along. Most memorable was the gig they played in a lucky fan's front yard as part of a Sydney radio station

H20 lead singer Toby Morse

"Live in Your Driveway" contest.

Good Charlotte then returned to the Northern Hemisphere to take on their very first headlining tour, the Uniting the States Tour with support acts Mest and the Movielife.

What to wish for for Christmas when all your dreams seem to be coming true? How about big screen dreams? Good Charlotte landed a slot on the *Not Another Teen Movie* soundtrack, released in December 2001. Featuring classic 80s tunes—many of which were hits when the punksters were just toddlers—reworked by some of the hottest bands of the New Millennium, the soundtrack was a hit. Anyone who has seen one of the original teen movies, *Sixteen Candles*, will remember the prom scene featuring OMD's "If You Leave"—the soppier of whom may even have misted up when the soaring strings hit their stride. Good Charlotte's version, needless to say, was a bit more upbeat. Other remakes include Marilyn Manson's driving electronic rendering of Soft Cell's "Tainted Love," Muse's cover of the Smiths' "Please, Please, Please Let Me Get What I Want," Goldfinger taking on Nena's "99 Red Luft Balloons," and adaptations of hits by the Pretenders (Saliva), New Order (Orgy and Stabbing Westward), Depeche Mode (Scott Weiland and Smashing Pumpkins), Modern English (Mest), and Jackson Browne (Phantom Planet). The brains behind this inspired collection were courtesy of Maverick Record's Guy Oseary, Madonna's whiz kid turned CEO and Executive Producer. Pretty cool, but even cooler still was the band's appearance in the movie itself. Good Charlotte got a chance to go to the prom after all.

FESTIVAL SONGS

BACK to summer camp! Good Charlotte joined up once again with a rotating roster of bands to take the 2002 Warped Tour on the road. Benji, Joel, Billy, and Paul were back in the fold with bands they had come to love to hang with, and got the opportunity to make even more friends in the rock world. The camaraderie and mutual respect between the performers was a large part of the unique ambiance of the tour. Mike Herrera of MxPx told *Billboard* in its June 22, 2002, issue,

"IT'S A GREAT TIME. THERE'S LOTS TO DO: PEOPLE TO MEET, OLD FRIENDS TO GET REACQUAINTED WITH. THERE'S ALWAYS BARBEQUES AND SOME KIND OF GAMBLING RACKET GOING ON."

Foregoing the conventional venues as usual, this year the tour set up camp in parking lots of arenas and amphitheatres, piers, fairgrounds, and even ski lodges.

Warped 2002 featured over forty bands, including Alkaline Trio, Bad Religion, the Casualties, the Damned, Eskimo Joe, Five Iron Frenzy, Flogging Molly, Good Charlotte, Glassjaw, Finch, Lagwagon, the Line, M16, Morgan Heritage, Mighty Mighty Bosstones, MxPx, New Found Glory, No Use for a Name, NOFX, Ozma, Planet Smashers, Recover, Reel Big Fish, Something Corporate, the Starting Line, Thrice, Tiger Amy, Total Chaos, Thursday, 28 Days, Good Charlotte favorites the Used, and Wanted Dead. In typical Warped spirit, there were curious standout musical acts including an Icelandic metal-rap hybrid named Quarashi, and the rather extraordinary accordion-and-glockenspiel-wielding World Inferno Friendship Society, vaguely reminiscent of a *Saturday Night Live* sketch.

The tour powered on from June 21 in Boise, Idaho, through August 18's Detroit, Michigan, finale. Aside from the Minneapolis show, which encountered a rather major glitch in the form of a violent storm that cut the power, the show sailed along smoothly. And in the high spirit of the event, no one let the lack of juice stop the fun; that night was rounded off acoustically.

In addition to all the rocking music, the eighth annual Warped surpassed its reputation for offering a vast array of entertainment. Attractions included the "Warped Are They Now?" museum, the Pirate Zone water game area, and Extreme Drumming contests in which concertgoers competed against speed records set by Warped drummers to win drum sets. Select stops on the tour hosted demos from the most talented up-and-coming skateboarders in custom-built skate arenas. Much to Good Charlotte's delight, there was an area dedicated exclusively to charities. Charity-supporting bands played here, and in between sets speakers from local nonprofit organizations left their booths and took the stage to speak to the crowds. The Ernie Ball Stage, a mainstay of the Warped Tour, brought the enterprising character of the festival to the forefront as hopeful new acts competed in the Ernie Ball Battle of the Bands. Winners went home happy—prizes included instruments, gear, and even recording contracts. The catchily entitled Balls of Steel was a show set inside a steel ball (ah-ha!) featuring three motorcyclists performing stunts all at once while incredibly managing not to mow each other down. What's missing from most testosterone-fueled punk fests? Why, the Ladies Lounge (now known as the Girlz Garage), where a girlfriend could get a little dose of fashion in the midst of all the moshing. Although why they should have a monopoly on the makeup tent isn't really clear—but they could always share the wealth with the guys after leaving the lounge. Rounding out the added attractions were a huge rock-climbing wall, water rides, a fanzine area, a customized button center, and loads of contests and giveaways.

The 2002 Warped tour was brought to you by Vans, Kevin Lyman, and Creative Artists Agency. Lyman, known for his well-organized, cost-effective production, once again conveyed that successful sensibility to the Warped Tour. Warped looks after its customers, providing locker areas to store that jacket your mom made you bring along with anything else you wish you didn't have to carry. Coolest of all by far was the Reverse Daycare—kids were able to drop their parents off guilt-free and enjoy the festivities without worrying for one minute: mom and dad were kept safe and sound in an air conditioned tent featuring movies, sound-proofed headphones, refreshments, and even masseuse services for those extra-stressed 'rents. Truly inspired.

There were a plethora of sponsors, including Sony PlayStation and Yoo-Hoo chocolate drinks as well as Vans. Detractors complained that the sponsors and exhibitors were selling out the punk-rock spirit, and some critics compared the festival to a corporate convention minus the suits and name badges, but the fans dismissed all that with a wave of their tattooed hands. At the end of the day, the tour broke its own prior 2001 record by bringing in a whopping $12 million and boasting over 500,000 satisfied attendees.

Good Charlotte found themselves with another major notch on their touring belt and a host of newly devoted fans. Indeed, their daily hour-long stint at the Meet and Greet tent was getting more and more crowded as the summer wore on. It certainly helped that the band had landed themselves a spot on the main stage this year, rather than on the decidedly lower-profile side stage of 2001's tour. In an amalgam of great live music, GC was definitely a Warped stand out.

ALL THINGS ROCK

GOOD CHARLOTTE'S rock and roll dreams were a definite reality. More and more opportunities were coming their way, and the guys didn't say no to any of them. In the midst of all the Warped excitement Benji and Joel had been appointed the first twin VJs in the history of MTV. With their own late-night video program called "All Things Rock," they were able to showcase little-known bands, and to turn young fans on to and educate them about the groups that came before Good Charlotte, like Social Distortion, Rancid, and NOFX. Although the twins didn't have complete control over the videos on the show, they managed to put their two cents worth in every chance they got.

Espousing a receptivity borne of their own experience, the twins know that the music world is a complex family tree of influences, and that young fans have to start somewhere. It was through reading interviews and liner notes of bands like Green Day and Rancid that Joel and Benji were turned on to the likes of the Clash, and they wanted to turn their own fans on to the fascinating and convoluted root system of rock. As Billy told *Billboard* on March 24, 2003,

"I DON'T THINK THAT WE ARE CHANGING THE TIMES. THE THING WITH OUR BAND IS WE KNOW WE'RE NOT DOING ANYTHING REVOLUTIONARY OR BRAND NEW IN MUSIC. SO, I THINK IT IS JUST TAKING INFLUENCES LIKE GREEN DAY AND STUFF, AND JUST ADDING THEM TO A LITTLE DIFFERENT STYLE OF MUSIC."

Joel discussed the MTV gig with the *Washington Times* in the paper's October 1, 2002, edition. "It's a lot of work, but it is a lot of fun because we've never really done TV before," he said. "It's been a really good experience. We play a lot of mainstream rock videos, but we also get to play a lot of stuff that you don't see all the time, like Glassjaw and New Found Glory." Benji and Joel are incredibly supportive of fellow musical artists, championing both old and new bands with sincere admiration. They may be musicians, but they are first and foremost music lovers, and their passion shines through. "Music is the one thing I believe in spending money on. It's the business I'm in, and I like supporting other artists," Joel told *Rolling Stone* in its November 21, 2002, edition. "I buy music every day. I try to support independent record stores and artists."

It seemed that Good Charlotte had accomplished everything they had worked so hard to achieve, and they could finally take a deep breath and come to the realization that indeed, everything was going to be all right.

"THIS PAST YEAR HAS BEEN THE FIRST YEAR OF MY LIFE WHERE I'VE BEEN TRULY HAPPY,"

Joel admitted to *Modern Fix* in July 2002. "Paul's known me since I was fifteen and I'm twenty-three now and he's seen it all, some major changes in my life. There isn't anything that can get me that down. Any problems you can have in a band, like not selling records, that doesn't bother me. I hope we sell records, but if we don't it won't break my heart. We're still going to make records and tour and be Good Charlotte. All those major problems that a lot of bands are always worried about really don't bother us because we're here now, and we got out of a really bad place so everything else is just like a bonus for us."

Benji and Joel headed back Down Under in September to do a little promotional representing. Hitting the TV airwaves, they got out the word about the forthcoming sophomore Good Charlotte album in advance of its October 7 Australian release date. The twins appeared on *The Panel* on September 11, Channel V's afternoon *whatuwant* show on September 12, and later that night performed live at Triple M studios for *Mosh Pit*. The band was becoming increasingly popular in Australia, and they held out hope that the new album would be a hit in what was one of their favorite countries in the world.

The Young and the Hopeless was released on October 1, 2002, in the United States and debuted at No. 7 on the *Billboard* charts. A dash of youth was just what was needed in a Top Ten topped by Elvis Presley and the Rolling Stones in the No. 1 and 2 slots. Despite once again less-than-ecstatic reviews (*Rolling Stone* declared it "strained" and stated that the twins "sometimes sound too desperate to establish their punker-than-thou credentials," and *Entertainment Weekly* complained, "These fourteen tidily produced songs not only sound a lot like each other, they also resemble ones by someone else—namely, Blink-182") the album was a definite hit. A hit with legs, as the next year would prove.

Never during the band's many early gigs at Washington's 9:30 Club could the guys of Good Charlotte have imagined that they would one day be celebrating the release of

their second major-label album there, but that's exactly what they did on October 1, 2002. Lucky fans who picked up a copy of *The Young and the Hopeless* at Tower Records in Rockville, Maryland, were given a free pass to the private 9:30 Club show.

The industry powers that be were enthusiastic and confident about Good Charlotte's potential. "The band and this album are in the right place at the right time," Chris Poppe, Epic's Vice President of Marketing, told *Billboard* in its September 28, 2002, issue. "People are starved for good rock music, and Good Charlotte delivers in spades. They knock people out with their live show. Their development and maturity as artists have broadened their scope of influence to encompass a wider, more diverse fan base. It's been great to see the excitement and support that has grown for the new album." David Massey, Executive Vice President of Epic Records and President of Daylight Records, summed up Good Charlotte's odds for success quite simply, saying, "These boys are poised to become one of the biggest young bands of the year. I wouldn't say something like that lightly." Apparently not, for indeed, the sort of bigtime, mainstream, platinum-record-selling, tour-headlining success that most bands daren't dream of was just around the corner for the hardworking boys from Maryland. Backed by A Fein Martini management team Steve Feinberg and Mike Martinovich and booked by Los Angeles's Creative Artists Agency, Good Charlotte was ready to hit the big time.

The Young and the Hopeless was produced by Eric Valentine, the man behind the sounds of Third Eye Blind, Smash Mouth, and Queens of the Stone Age. Valentine apparently believes in doing his homework. He spent time with the guys in Washington, D.C., checking out their haunts—hanging at their favorite tattoo parlor and drinking in their local pubs. As Benji told *MTV News* on October 4, 2002, "Basically, he wanted to see where we grew up, what we do when we're home, who we hang out with and just get our vibe. We owe him a lot because he really understood what we wanted to do so we were definitely on the same page." The album was recorded at Eric's own Barefoot Studios in Los Angeles, which afforded the band the freedom to record when they wanted for as long as they wanted since they weren't slaves to pre-booked recording blocks.

The album features Josh Freese, previously of the Vandals and Perfect Circle, on drums. The band still hadn't found a permanent replacement for Aaron and had been working with a revolving roster of drummers on tour.

"I think this album really captures how much we've grown and learned about music," Paul says on the CD extra. "I used over nine basses on this album. On the last album I did it all with one bass. I'm, like, actually proud to show this CD to other musicians."

"We really pushed ourselves on this one," Joel told Australian magazine *Blunt* in its September 2002 issue. "We wrote a bunch of songs that we threw away, because they were all just pop punk songs, and we didn't want to just make another record like the last one. We pulled out a bunch of our favorite records and really tried to work out what we liked about them. And so we tried to write each song not to be catchy, but to stand alone."

CHANGE

THE YOUNG AND THE HOPELESS's first single, "Lifestyles of the Rich and the Famous," was an instant hit with modern rock radio. The song's video, directed by Bill Fishman, was a high-rotation MTV darling and a TRL favorite, and deservedly so. Fishman, the man behind classic punk clips for the likes of Suicidal Tendencies and the Ramones—including the landmark "I Wanna Be Sedated" video—hadn't worked on a music video for years, as he now favored motion picture work, and his comeback to the genre was a success. The video featured some surprising cameo appearances. Tenacious D's Kyle Gass, punk-rock icon Mike Watt (bass player for Minutemen and Firehose), and *NSYNC member Chris Kirkpatrick starring as Chadwick Merriweather Harding III rounded out the cast. Wait a minute—*NSYNC?! Good Charlotte first met up with *NSYNC in 2001, and struck up what might initially seem an unlikely friendship. As Benji owned up to *MTV News* on August 26, 2002, "I went in with a bad attitude. I figured, 'Awww, these guys are d---s. I'm just gonna glom them.' And they just turned out to be the coolest, nicest guys. It really made me think twice about people in general." The video proved itself an MTV fave, and had to be retired with honors from TRL after hitting the limit of fifty days.

"Lifestyles" broke into the Billboard Hot 100 at the beginning of December at No. 61, joining the esteemed and varied company of Eminem's "Lose Yourself," Missy Misdemeanor Eliott's "Work It," and "Jenny from the Block" by the ubiquitous J.Lo in the top three slots. The top debut on the Hot 100 charts, the track also slid in at a very respectable No. 11 on the Modern Rock Tracks chart. The tune, with its Iggy Pop "Lust for Life" drumbeat and a chorus that will stick in your mind all day long (*Lifestyles of the rich and the famous / They're always complaining, always complaining / If money is such a problem / Well they got mansions / Think we should rob*

them) was a rocking, rousing hit.

"It's kind of a social commentary," Benji explained to *Teen People* on April 18, 2003. "With that song, well, we've noticed how a lot of famous people can get away with anything they want. Whether you're having success in music or film or whatever, you should count your blessings instead of whining about everything. When we were coming up, we'd see bands complaining or throwing their careers away with drugs and stuff like that, and we'd be like, 'We'll take your place! Give us a shot.' If you don't want to do it, step off and let some kid that's coming up take your place."

Joel told *Billboard* in its September 28, 2002, edition, "Since the first album, we've become better at articulating our feelings and thoughts as a band. We want the listeners to be able to relate to us on a personal level. We aren't role models; we are mirrors for our listeners. We don't complain; we just lay it out there. We are tired of hearing bands teaching hate. We care about what our fans get out of our music." Joel's apparent growth as a songwriter is certainly showcased on the new album, and although he recognizes that growth, he remains modest and realizes that it is an ongoing process. "I always feel like there's songs inside that I know just aren't ready to come out because I'm not good enough yet," he told Sony's Australian website on November 21, 2002. "I think with this record I can articulate what I'm thinking better. I think those songs came out at a perfect time, because it was that time for us with this record to go a little to other places, open some more doors. I've worked hard on the lyrics. We always hope as a band to grow and I think that this record really shows that we did."

"My Bloody Valentine" is perhaps a good example of the twins' creative development. "The song is more of a poem," Benji explained to *MTV News* on October 4, 2002. "It's a story about a love triangle, but it's got a real Edgar Allan Poe vibe to it. . . . It's definitely different than anything we've ever done and that's one reason we like it so much. It's something we couldn't

*NSYNC member Chris Kirkpatrick

have written four years ago."

The brothers were still working through their father's betrayal through their music. "The Story of My Old Man" addresses his drinking (*Last I heard he was at the bar doing himself in / I know I got that same disease, I guess I got that from him*). Benji—who battled with his own drinking demons in the early touring days, ending up in fist fights with anyone who dared question his punk status—is now a proud recovering alcoholic who has been clean for a long time. Although Good Charlotte is suspected by some to be proponents of the strict "straight-edge" school of

No Doubt

punk that bans drugs and alcohol, the other band members don't object to indulging in the odd beer, but out of respect for Benji they won't do so in his company. "We live pretty much the anti-rock-and-roll cliché," Billy admits to *Rolling Stone* in its May 1, 2003, cover story on the band. "We're supposed to tell you about all of our drug problems and all this stuff. But, unfortunately, we don't have any."

The twins composed "Emotionless," an open letter of sorts to their father, together, and in it they admit to missing the man who walked out of their lives. Sadly their father still had not shown any interest in his sons; Benji recalled to *Rolling Stone* in the magazine's May 1, 2003, cover story how, when he was nineteen, he attempted to reach out to his father. "I was willing to put it all aside. And basically he was like, 'I'm trying to start a new life. I'm trying to forget about you guys.' The last time I ever talked to him was on the phone that day."

Yet another deeply emotional track on the album is "Hold On," an anti-suicide song. Joel was inspired to write the uplifting lyrics after receiving hundreds of letters from fans claiming that Good Charlotte's music had helped them through the darkest of times.

Good Charlotte enjoyed a spate of media attention following the album's release, notably making the cover of *Alternative Press* magazine's November 2002 edition with its witty byline, "Punk and Disorderly:

Behind the Sugar and Spikes of Good Charlotte." The band was voted straight to the top in the 2002 A.P. Reader's Poll, winning Best Artist, Artist with Most Integrity, and Best CD for *The Young and the Hopeless*. TV appearances on *Late Night with Conan O'Brien* on October 5 and on *Last Call with Carson Daly* on November 19 gave the band a spot of late-night exposure.

In their usual energetic style, Good Charlotte hopped the pond to the U.K. for a quick bit of promotion at the beginning of October. The trip gave the twins the opportunity to visit Ireland. The band returned to the U.S.A. to join Gwen Stefani and the boys of No Doubt as their support band for a few dates of the North American tour for the album *Rock Steady*, playing October 9, 2002, in St. Paul, Minnesota; the 11th in Rosemont, Illinois; the 12th in Detroit; and the 14th in State College, Pennsylvania. Also playing as support were the Distillers. Garbage took over Good Charlotte's slot on October 15. "We tried to get the whole tour," Paul told *Livewire* magazine on August 11, 2002. "But those are the only shows we could get. I think it's awesome. . . . It's always good to get exposed to people that haven't heard you. . . . You can't really expand your audience when you're playing by yourself. No Doubt plays arenas, so there should be a lot of people there, and we hope it goes well."

On October 15, 2002, the guys launched their very own headlining month-long expedition at the Buffalo, New York, Showplace. The audiences had all managed to memorize all of the songs on the brand new album and sang along with the band at every show until the last date on November 15 in Orlando, Florida.

Good Charlotte then leapfrogged to the Boom Boom Huck Jam tour, the brainchild of skateboarding guru and many-time medalist of ESPN's X Games Tony Hawk. An extreme sports festival featuring skateboarding, biking, and motocross, Huck Jam's arenas were made up of a huge network of custom-built ramps and sets for sporting exhibitions. One musical act performed at each event; most stayed with the tour for several days and then passed the gig on to their punk colleagues. The Offspring took the start date of October 12 in San Jose, California. Face to Face played a few gigs, followed by Devo, CKY, and Social Distortion. Good Charlotte's stint comprised three dates: November 14 in Atlanta, Georgia; November 16 in Tampa, Florida; and November 17 in Sunrise, Florida. Sponsored by Activision, MTV2, PlayStation 2, and Squeeze 'n Go pudding, the tour was a sort of warped Warped—a Warped in reverse, with sports taking the main stage and music a supporting role.

Good Charlotte turned up in the U.K. again just as Americans were getting ready to celebrate Thanksgiving, with gigs in London at The Garage on November 22, in Scotland at Glasgow's G2 on the 23rd, and at Liverpool University on the 24th. They supported Our Lady Peace on the 28th at the University of London Union, a basement pub venue that had hosted many up-and-coming bands over the years. The GC gang was making solid strides toward getting the word out to the British.

The usual rash of Christmas musical fests brought to all the good little boys and girls by their favorite local radio stations in 2002 featured more than a few stocking-stuffers for Good Charlotte fans. The band performed at the December 5 KDGE-FM's How the Edge Stole Christmas concert in the Dallas, Texas, Bronco Bowl along with Everclear, Three Doors Down, and Sum 41. Three days later they turned up in Los Angeles at the two-day annual KROQ Almost Acoustic Christmas at the Universal Amphitheater which boasted quite a lineup: Audioslave, Coldplay, Creed, Dashboard Confessional, Disturbed, *SNL's* Jimmy Fallon, Good Charlotte, Jack Johnson, Jurassic 5, New Found Glory, P.O.D., Queens of the Stone Age, Sum 41, Taproot, Trust Company, the Vines, the Used, and Billy Corgan's Zwan. December 11 found the Good Charlotte guys in Denver, Colorado, for KTCL-FM's Not So Silent Night gig in the company of Authority Zero, Bowling for Soup, and Unwritten Law. The next day they hit Seattle, Washington, for KNDD-FM's Deck the Hall Ball with Disturbed, Sum 41, Three Doors Down, and Sparta. On to San Jose, California, on the 13th for yet another Not So Silent Night, this time brought to you by KITS-FM and featuring DJ Shadow, the Donnas, Disturbed, Moby, and Paper Roach. A cross-country flight put the band in Pittsburgh, Pennsylvania, the very next day with Punchline and Sum 41 at the WXDX-FM Kick Ass Xmas concert. December 15 was slated for Philadelphia's WPLY-FM Feastival, where Good Charlotte shared the stage with Coldplay, New Found Glory, Queens of the Stone Age, Seether, and Zwan. Anything But Joey, the Distillers, Jimmy Eat World, OK Go, and SR-71 were their contemporaries in Kansas City for KRBZ-FM's Happy Birthday Jesus Christmas Party on the 16th. The nonstop yuletide cheer motored on to finale in Detroit, Michigan, on the 18th when Good Charlotte joined up with Box Car Racer, New Found Glory, Trust Co., the Vines, the Used, and Zwan for the CIMX's the Night 89X Stole Christmas. And you thought Christmas shopping was tiring! This rock lifestyle was hard work, and Good Charlotte loved every minute of it.

DON'T WANNA BE JUST LIKE YOU

SANTA was making his list, but Good Charlotte barely had time for sleeping, much less shopping. They had to prepare for their performance at MTV's New Year's Eve show to be broadcast live from Times Square in New York City. They also had to fit in the filming in Los Angeles of the video for their next single, "The Anthem."

MTV News quoted Joel on December 13, 2002, describing the "The Anthem" video as "Just like a big party, kind of showing who we are and our whole culture that we live in, our own little world. And it's kind of like celebrating that we don't really want to adhere to or fulfill the status quo way of life, I guess the average thing you're taught—to, like, grow up and get a job. We're kind of showing our side of our kind of culture." Featuring the band's friends, the band's friends' cars, and the band's friends' dogs, the clip is directed by the band's peers Smith N' Borin, the team GC met during Warped and who are also responsible for videos by Bowling for Soup and Simple Plan. "Anthem," with its antiestablishment theme (*Go to college, a university / Get a real job that's what they said to me*) encourages kids to be themselves and go against the flow.

"The Anthem" isn't just about high school," Joel explained to VH-1 on April 4, 2003. "It's about everyone that doesn't want to have that status-quo lifestyle where they go to college, get a job, get a house and two cars, and a wife and two kids. High school is a part of that, because that's where they teach you how to be the rest of your life. I hated high school. The song's aimed at kids who want to be different and do something like be a band." The song was the top debut in the Billboard Hot 100 singles chart headed by 50 Cent and R. Kelly, coming in at No. 56, and went on to be featured on the EA Sports *Madden NFL 2003* video game. The song proved itself popular in England as well, and the U.K.'s *Dot Music* gave it a nine out of ten, raving, "the Madden Bros. Express has gathered such a head of steam no one can stop it. Throw those hands up and live a little; after all, the break at two minutes twenty-seven seconds alone must make it a contender for rock single of the year."

The New Year's Eve MTV gig went off without a hitch. On December 31, 2002, Good Charlotte performed "Lifestyles of the Rich and the Famous" live during the Pajama Jam Party. Joel gave a shout out to his punk colleagues New Found Glory, MxPx, and others.

Some like Paris in spring, but Good Charlotte opted for Japan in January. They toured the country along with New Found Glory and found

themselves with yet another legion of new fans.

In mid January 2003, Good Charlotte was featured on MTV and *MTV2's Spankin' New Bands* feature along with the Donnas, New Found Glory, Simple Plan, and the Used. The combination of a one-song live set on MTV's *Total Request Live* (*TRL* to those in the know) and a half-hour gig on MTV2 was to bring new music to the masses, and it worked like a charm. The exposure certainly seemed to do the trick, as all five bands saw their albums climb the charts immediately after the shows aired. Good Charlotte jumped from No. 25 to No. 12 on the Billboard album charts, and made a good showing on the Top Pop Catalog Albums chart with a leap from No. 18 to No. 4 earning the band the "Greatest Gainer" credit.

The Good Charlotte gang was excited to make another transatlantic trip to England in February, as the British were begrudgingly admitting to a weakness for the Maryland band. Despite labeling Good Charlotte "U.S. pretty boy pop punksters" who have been "causing ripples of excitement amongst screaming girlies and angsty boys all over the U.S.," longstanding U.K. music mag *Kerrang!* graciously conceded in its January 8, 2003, edition that, "unlike the usual dumb-ass punk pop japery peddled by so many bands currently on the scene, Good Charlotte manage to do it with substance, style, and an occasional deeper exploration of sociopolitical themes." Another venerable publication, *NME* (*New Music Express*) gave *The Young and the Hopeless* an eight out of ten rating, and went as far as to say that "within these standard-issue Angsty sk8er Bois lurks an emo-esque intelligence that'd kill Blink-182 in under a minute were they infected with it" and goes on to portray "Lifestyles of the Rich and the Famous" as "advocat[ing] an anarchistic form of rob-the-rich Communism while taking sideswipes at celebrity culture, political hypocrisy, and OJ Simpson. The title track is an earnest reevaluation of the very term 'punk.'" Praise indeed for a band whose punk values are all to often brought into question.

They returned Stateside just in time to perform on the *Tonight Show with Jay Leno* on February 24, and then turned around to take off once again, this time leaving the U.S.A. to head back down to Australia for the fourth time. The affection the band feels toward that part of the world is returned in kind by the ever-expanding multitude of Australian fans. Consistently topping the ARIA charts with every single they've released since "Little Things," the band seemed to have struck a chord in the sunbaked land. They rocked Queensland at their February 27 all-ages show at the Brisbane Arena. A March 1 gig at Sydney's Enmore Theatre followed. The band got the most out of Sydney by hitching a ride on Channel V's *Music Bus* on March 2, enabling them to play a free oceanside gig at the city's Cronulla Beach. The next day they did an in-store appearance at Sydney's Mid City Centre HMV, meeting Aussie fans and signing CDs. Good Charlotte next showed up in Adelaide for a March 5 concert at the Barton Theatre and the next night played Melbourne's Festival Hall. Fans who couldn't make it to one of these major cities were treated to a live performance of "The Anthem" on Aussie TV's *Rove Live* on March 4. The GC team then hopped over to New Zealand to film the video for their next single "Girls and Boys."

WALDORF WORLDWIDE

GOOD **C**HARLOTTE'S profile was climbing higher and higher. On April 5, 2003, they were the musical guests on *Saturday Night Live*, hosted that week by funnyman Bernie Mac; their live performances of "The Anthem" and "Lifestyles of the Rich and the Famous" rocked the set. They then hit the touring highway again as co-headliners with New Found Glory on the third annual Honda Civic Tour. Previous years' tours had featured bigtime groups Blink-182, Everclear, and Incubus. The 2003 tour, co-sponsored by MTV's *TRL*, stopped off at amphitheaters and arenas to play a total of forty-seven dates throughout the spring. An ironic twist saw Good Charlotte and New Found Glory being supported by the very bands that had given them their own starts as support acts—MxPx and Less than Jake. Although from the outside it may have seemed a bit odd for the older acts to see their young upstart protégés turn the tables as headliners, these bands were friends and supported one another, no matter who was more popular. The combination worked out very well, as longtime Good Charlotte fans were very familiar with MxPx music from the early touring days. Less than Jake took the first leg of the tour, supporting at gigs from April 8 through May 4. On May 6 MxPx took over for the second leg. A short list of groups—the Disasters, Hot Rod Circuit, the Movielife, and Stretch Arm Strong—played as the opening fourth band at select concerts.

The guys of Good Charlotte showcased their typically positive and enthusiastic attitude at a press conference before the tour. Benji told *MTV News* on February 25, 2003, "I want to point out how impressed I am with Honda, just being able to see the scene we're involved in. There's not many companies that would want to be involved in the culture that we're in at a major level like this, so we're all very surprised." Joel cracked, "I heard all the presidents of Honda are getting tattoos."

As if a joint show from these two bands wasn't enough, there were a few goodies to be won. NFG gave contest-winners stage-side bleacher seats throughout the tour. A wish come true to a crowd made up of young fans fresh out of driver's ed, twelve customized Hondas were given away through the concerts to the young fans. Two of the vehicles were actually customized by NFG and GC, and the Charlotte-mobile was an orange, black, and neon-green creation with "Hopeless" painted on the sides.

The first date of the Civic Tour was in Grand Forks, North Dakota, on April 8. The double-header barreled its way across the United States, making the day of fans in Alabama, Arizona, Colorado, Connecticut, Florida, Georgia, Idaho, Illinois, Indiana, Kansas, Louisiana, Maine, Massachusetts, Michigan, Minnesota, Missouri, Nebraska, Nevada, New Jersey, New York, North Carolina (in Charlotte, of course!), Ohio, Oregon, Pennsylvania, South Carolina, Texas, Utah, Virginia, Washington, Washington D.C., and Wisconsin, with the final gig at the Universal Amphitheatre in Los Angeles on June 7. Taking turns at the first and second slots each night, Good Charlotte and New Found Glory proved themselves to be perfect complements to one another. Of course, the fact that the two bands are close buddies whose careers had been on parallel tracks for the past few years didn't hurt. As NFG lead singer Jordan Pundik told *Rolling Stone* in its February 25, 2003, edition, "We're like best friends now. It's just better to tour with your friends." The mutual admiration between the two bands manifests itself even on band members' skin; Jordan proudly sports a Good Charlotte tattoo and Billy has an NFG tattoo on his leg. Now that's true friendship. Known to represent not only his favorite bands on his body (a Silverchair tattoo was an early one), Billy also exhibits a Lord of the Rings ring tattooed on one finger, and a *Nightmare before Christmas* on his right arm.

Critics continued to slight the pop-punk stars, but it was the fans' euphoric reception that fueled Good Charlotte's sets. The *New York Times* concert review of the NYC gig in Manhattan's Hammerstein Ballroom started out in the obligatory negative vein. "Some people call it 'mall punk,' a subgenre ruled by polite, energetic bands that sometimes seem to have been concocted in an MTV laboratory," the May 3, 2003, review read. It goes on to confess, "The term is invariably used as an insult, even though the bands themselves are generally unobjectionable: they make memorable videos, they write catchy songs and as Good Charlotte and New Found Glory proved on Tuesday night they can get thousands of kids to sing along." Exactly. Indeed, reviewers across the country rarely failed to be impressed with the audience's obvious adoration of Good Charlotte and their music, and almost every review cited with apparent disbelief that the crowd sang along to every word all night long.

The Good Charlotte concert experience is also remarkable for its distinct lack of aggro. The crowd may be pogoing away, but nary a foot is stepped on. A heightened sense of punk-rock bonhomie prevails. A prepubescent who triumphantly body surfs his way into the security pit is effortlessly hoisted away by a bodyguard—not to be bodily evicted from the premises but rather to be gently returned to his place in the audience. All is right with the world for a couple of hours.

It is often said that performers and audiences feed off one another. At a Good Charlotte gig, it is impossible to say who is having more fun: the fans or the band. "I think my favorite moment at a concert is the, like, five seconds before you walk on stage," Billy says on *The Young and the Hopeless* CD Extra. "The lights go off and the crowd cheers and they're ready and then it hits you, like, yeah, this is awesome. You know, like that's the moment every night that it hits me and I'm like, that's why I love this."

Good Charlotte are not into the ego-enhancing encore scene, either. They give the fans what they want and say goodnight, leaving them satisfied without having to scream and beg for the "surprise" reappearance of the big rock stars. The Who's "Baba O'Reilly" with its apropos "teenage wasteland" chorus was Good Charlotte's send-them-home lights-on track of choice this time around.

The tour was virtually nonstop, but the band took a few short breaks. On May 5 Benji and Joel hosted the Acoustic Benefit for Positive Force at Philadelphia's Theatre of Living Arts. The D.C.-based charity provides aid to the elderly and homeless. The twins also took the stage for a half-hour acoustic set along with support performances by Army of Me and Ben Lee. The band managed to sandwich in a May appearance on *Late Night with David Letterman* in which Joel and Benji exchanged a little shoulder slapping with Dave himself.

Later that month the GC crew had another hiatus in between their May 23 gig at Colorado's famed Red Rocks and their May 26 stop-off in Seattle. Ah yes, a little R&R, a short holiday hanging by the pool. . .uh, no, not for Good Charlotte. The break from playing on tour gave them a chance to play on yet another stage—one they may have felt they owed a little favor. The WHFS Festival, a major supporter of Good Charlotte when they were unknown up-and-comers, was treated on May 24 to hometown heroes made good. Amongst the thirty other bands performing at the Washington, D.C., festivities were Blur and Godsmack.

The Good Charlotte/New Found Glory outing was a resounding success according to fans, the band, and the industry alike. Selling out venues that normally play host to the Rolling Stones is not an easy task, but they managed it date after date. Providing kids not much younger than themselves with a good night out was a straightforward, respectable goal, and the two bands pulled it off with pop-punk aplomb. Joel expressed his view to the *Washington Post* in its November 12, 2000, edition, saying simply, "Music is supposed to be an escape. It's supposed to be somewhere you go, where you can be yourself, or be whatever you want to be. Above anything that happens, we want kids who come see us for that hour to totally forget about high school, to totally forget about everything, to just have an awesome time."

Milking a huge paycheck out of the touring business was not on the agenda either, and Good Charlotte didn't have trouble convincing their management that pleasing the fans was what it was all about. Ticket prices were kept around the $25 range. "We could definitely make more money by creeping up the price," the band's manager Steve Feinberg openly allows to *Billboard* in its August 30, 2003, issue. "But most of our fans are under twenty and work crappy jobs. We would rather have another fan than squeeze out another dollar."

GIRLS & BOYS

SPEAKING of fans, Good Charlotte's fan base continued to grow by leaps and bounds, and as a testament to their far-reaching appeal, managed to encompass not only the high school, college, and early-twenties slice of the pie, but also laid claim to the preteen segment of society. The Good Charlotte guys probably never envisioned themselves in the company of the likes of Ashton Kutcher, Hilary Duff, Justin Timberlake, and Beyonce Knowles, but that's exactly what can be found on the glossy cover of the October 2003 issue of longtime teen 'zine *Tiger Beat*. A British publication aimed at teenaged girls across the United Kingdom, *J17* ("The Mag that Goes Faster! Every month!") labels Good Charlotte's style "Colorful. Quirky. Cute." and the band's sound as "Kick-ass sing-along rock." *J17* goes on to explain, "mad hair and great makeup aside, we love these lads for their deeply personal, totally honest, and fantastically funny lyrics."

Many bands find the "teeny-bop" connection to be a hard-to-shake curse of sorts, but Good Charlotte is able to pull it off without breaking a sweat. They adore every last one of their fans, and it simply wouldn't occur to them to adopt an elitist attitude. Why not have the respect of hardcore established punk peers while at the same time garnering the kind of attention that warrants a feature entitled "Go on a Date with Good Charlotte" in which young readers are invited to imagine what a date with each band member would be like? Or a feature in *Bop* magazine in which a "body language expert" analyzes photos of the band to reveal the true natures of Joel and Benji's personalities? Really, why not? O.K., England's "Just for Teens" magazine *J-14* boasting Good Charlotte cutout finger puppets in its October/November 2003 issue might be pushing the cute envelope, but hey, this band is just so darn likeable that no one can be bothered to begrudge them their universal magnetism. In fact, even parents were beginning to admit to approval of the tattooed punks with the catchy tunes.

Good Charlotte may have unbelievably dedicated fans, but rarely do you see a band so devoted to their fans. No matter how famous the band was becoming, the GC guys were determined to keep it real. Radio station DJs expressed disbelief at the amount of time the band was willing to spend outside talking to camped-out fans, sometimes missing their time slot on the air.

The GC guys do admit to being a bit flabbergasted at all the female attention, however. They may be faced with trembling, crying young women bearing homemade gifts these days, but it's all a far cry from their past experience with the opposite sex, and they treat it with dubious bemusement. Paul scoffs "No one has a crush on the *bass player*!" on *The Young and the Hopeless* CD-extra. When a female fan sporting the requisite

Good Charlotte T-shirt gushes, "Good Charlotte's the best band—I love you guys so much!" the camera pans to Joel who says, "We take that to heart, ha ha ha!" and then quickly begins singing some Morrissey to create a diversion. Benji, too, seems cynical about any newfound advantages on the love life front.

"WHEN A GIRL'S DAD IS LIKE, 'SO, WHAT DO YOU DO?' AND YOU SAY, 'I'M IN A ROCK BAND,' YOU CAN FEEL INFERIOR,"

he told *Teen People* in its May 12, 2003, "25 Hottest Under 25" feature. Despite their skepticism, the fact is that these punks have managed to attain a boy-band level of female devotion that forces them to resort to using security-surrounded cabs to transport them the short distance from their tour bus to the door.

But enough about the fairer sex. Good Charlotte had too much to do to worry about their love lives. They lent their music to yet another good cause on June 3, 2003, when the *Liberation Songs to Benefit PETA* CD was released. PETA (People for the Ethical Treatment of Animals) had joined forces with the Fat Wreck Chords label to put together the sixteen-track compilation featuring Goldfinger, NOFX, the Used, and others. An acoustic version of "Lifestyles of the Rich and the Famous" is featured on the disc, which sold for under $5. The animal rights issue has always been close to the band's heart; they had begun handing out pro-vegetarian and antivivisection pamphlets at their shows that spring. Billy, a staunch vegetarian, expressed his views to PETA2 in an interview, saying, "Animals can't talk, you know, and if you are going to kill another person, they're going to be like, 'No, don't kill me!' If you are gonna kill an animal, no one speaks for the animals. Someone's got to do it . . . my message would be that they are living a life, too. You can survive totally fine with not eating animals. You might as well just not eat them, so it's kind of simple. Let people speak for the animals and just live normally, that's how I feel about it. I think the biggest part is, I have a million pets—I have cats, dogs, spiders—I couldn't imagine eating my pets. Why would I eat any other animals? You can survive totally fine without eating animals, so I don't think that you should."

Canada's MuchMusic Video Awards took place on June 22, 2003, at the Toronto headquarters of the music channel. Good Charlotte's "Anthem" was nominated along with videos by Audioslave, Coldplay, Disturbed, Linkin Park, the Music, Queens of the Stone Age, System of a Down, Weezer, and the White Stripes for the "Best International Video–Group." However, once again it was the fans themselves that ensured Benji, Billy, Joel, and Paul a win, voting them in as the "People's Choice: Favorite International Group," over Coldplay, Linkin Park, Red Hot Chili Peppers, and the White Stripes.

"Girls and Boys" was pulled out of the hat as the third single from *The Young and the Hopeless*, and debuted on the Billboard Hot 100 singles chart at No. 75 in mid July. The Smith N' Borin–directed video, shot earlier that year in New Zealand, is as raucous as the song itself, featuring a backyard picnic and a punked-out grandma in the mosh pit. The video for "The Young and the Hopeless," the next single, is equally as much fun, featuring the band rocking out in a tiny room as medals, trophies, framed certificates, and rosettes are knocked off shelves and walls in true punk fashion.

Good Charlotte decided to forego Warped 2003, instead opting to concentrate on expanding their profile abroad by playing many of the major summer festivals in Europe and Japan. The band played Japan's Summer Sonic 2003 along with an exceptional selection of both up-and-coming and veteran acts including AFI, Alkaline Trio, Blink-182, Blondie, My Morning Jacket, New Found Glory, and Radiohead. Their appearance at the U.K.'s Reading Festival was met with mixed reviews, but all in all the summer was a scorcher, and more and more girls and boys were jumping on the Good Charlotte bandwagon.

LIFESTYLES OF THE PUNK
AND THE FAMOUS

GOOD CHARLOTTE was hotter than ever, popping up all over the place in various extracurricular activities. On July 16 the band participated in yet another MTV venture when they opened the *AT&T Wireless Presents Hard Rock Live* program filmed in Orlando, Florida. You know you've made it when other bands invite you to collaborate with them on new projects, and Benji began making guest appearances in spades. He joined in on the punk-reggae band Morgan Heritage's single "Jump Around" as well as on Chicago band Mest's single "Jaded (These Years)," the band's first single on their third Maverick Records album. Sporting a new pink and black leopard hairstyle, Benji turned up on the "Jaded" video, a house-party themed clip featuring the requisite motorcycle/beer can stunt along with a touch of nudity (no, not our Benj!). Benji also lent his vocals to Goldfinger's new single "January" on the *Open Your Eyes* album. But it wasn't only Benji who was in demand. Joel sang along with Simple Plan's Pierre on the "You Don't Mean Anything" track on the *No Pads, No Helmets. . . Just Balls* album. The whole band lent their pop-punk power to yet another teen movie on the soundtrack companion CD to the third installment in Universal's *American Pie* film series, *American Wedding*. Released on July 22, the CD featured the track "The Anthem," and also included "Forget Everything," a previously unreleased song from New Found Glory, as well as tunes from the Foo Fighters, Avril Lavigne, Sugarcult, and the Wallflowers.

Rock stars, TV stars, movie stars . . . these guys could do it all. So why not give Calvin Klein a run for his money and give fashion design a try? Benji and Joel's MADE label's line of sweatshirts, T-shirts, bandanas, underwear, and—don't feel left out, girls—a women's selection, were

available at Hot Topic stores and online at madeclothing.com. Billy also started up a ready-to-wear collection, calling his line of Level 27 Clothing, "Clothing for the Children of the Night." Professing to cater to all varieties of music fans, from punks to metal heads to hip-hop lovers to goth to skater to graffiti kids, his clothes were also being sold in Hot Topic stores and on level27online.com. Billy's artistic tendencies led him to create himself a shirt sporting his lucky number and he went from there. As a kid, he was obsessed with drawing. As he recalled to *Overated* magazine on August 14, 2002, "I used to just watch cartoons. Sit in front of the TV and watch cartoons with a piece of paper and a pencil. I would draw every cartoon character. I wanted to work for Disney really bad and be an animator. I'd sit around and draw all day long. I never really went out and played in the woods with a bunch of snakes under rocks. I was scared of snakes. I was pretty little so I would just sit around and draw. That's all I really did."

Good Charlotte made a good showing at the 2003 Teen Choice

Awards. The August 6 live ceremony was truly for teenagers only—votes were placed by those aged thirteen through nineteen via America Online and TeenPeople.com for the whopping fifty-six categories in TV, music, movies, sports, and even video games. Jennifer Lopez and Eminem vied for the most nominations, even finding themselves up against one another in the best movie lip lock category. But it was Good Charlotte who stole the show in the music categories. Knocking Christina Aguilera, 50 Cent, Avril Lavigne, John Mayer, J.Lo, and Justin Timberlake out of the ring in the Teen Choice Music Album competition, *The Young and the Hopeless* triumphed. They were also nominated for Teen Choice Rock Group alongside Audioslave, Coldplay, Linkin Park, No Doubt, Sum 41, Three Doors Down, and the White Stripes.

Yet another award show was close on the heels of the Teen Choice— what's a rock star to do?—this time in London. Good Charlotte jetted over to the U.K. to pick up an award for Best Single for "Lifestyles of the Rich and the Famous" and perform at the *Kerrang!* Awards. The August 21 ceremony took place at the Royal Lancaster Hotel and featured the inauguration of Metallica into the Hall of Fame. Other award-winners were the Red Hot Chili Peppers, Linkin Park, and Evanescence.

Good Charlotte couldn't linger in the United Kingdom to celebrate their win, however, as they had to hurry home for the much-anticipated 2003 MTV Video Music Awards held on August 28 in New York City's Radio Music Hall. The always entertaining show, once again this year MC'd by the hilarious and irreverent Chris Rock, and this year featuring the Britney/Madonna make-out session, is a notch in the belt to any band or artist invited to perform. Good Charlotte did not disappoint. They went home happy with their "Anthem" performance, and happy with their nominations for "Best Group Video" and "Best Rock Video" for "Lifestyles of the Rich and the Famous," although they lost to Coldplay's "The Scientist" and Linkin Park's "Somewhere I Belong" respectively. Of course, knocking Beyonce/Jay-Z, American Idol Kelly Clarkson, Eminem, and Justin Timberlake out of the ring to win a coveted moon man for the "Viewer's Choice" award wasn't too bad either!

There's no place like home, and Good Charlotte happily agreed to rock good old Washington, D.C., once more. The band helped Aerosmith, Mary J. Blige, Aretha Franklin, and Britney Spears inaugurate the new National Football League season on September 5, 2003, at the "NFL Kickoff Live" extravaganza held on the Washington, D.C., Mall.

It was now time to hit the big time on the road: Good Charlotte was ready to launch their very own full-blown headlining tour. With *The Young and the Hopeless* now certified at double platinum status and kids clamoring for more opportunities to see the band's kicking live show, the GC crew decided to do what they do best and bring their music directly to their fans. The band determined to keep ticket prices in the $25 range and planned to give their fans both new and old a night to remember.

The opening dates put aside any doubt as to whether Good Charlotte could carry its own major tour. The crowds were going mad well before the massive banner depicting *The Young and the Hopeless* album cover lifted to reveal the band playing "A New Beginning." An advantage to the band headlining on their own was that they had more time on stage, and they took the extra time to offer up a more diverse range of material. A true highlight of this tour was Benji and Joel's acoustic version of "Thank You Mom."

Originally slated opening act the Living End from Australia were forced to pull out of the tour due to a U.S. customs visa hold-up. Taking their place were trio Saving Face and piano-driven rockers Something Corporate, whose lead singer, Andrew McMahon, before launching into a ballad one night, humorously warned the crowd, "If you haven't heard us before and don't like us, this might be a good time to go to the bathroom!"

Good Charlotte continued to deliver the kicking live shows their fans had come to expect.

"EVEN WHEN WE'RE IN THE STUDIO, WE'RE THINKING ABOUT HOW THE SONGS WILL WORK ON STAGE. WE CONSCIOUSLY ADD PARTS THAT WILL BE GOOD SINGALONG MOMENTS, OR BUILD-UPS TO GET THE CROWD WORKING,"

Billy revealed in an October 16, 2001, Sony Music Canada interview.

NO FUTURE?!?

WHAT does the future hold for Good Charlotte? One thing's for sure: they aren't taking anything for granted, and although they could be branded both rich and famous, they are the last to buy into that lifestyle. You won't find Benji and Joel lounging poolside at the Playboy mansion or blowing their royalty checks on Bentleys and bling-bling. When the band started earning serious money, the first thing the twins did was to buy their mom a house. The only luxuries that interest the GC guys are top musical gear. Benji sticks to custom-made guitars courtesy of Ernie Ball Music Man and Randall amps. Chris's drums of choice are Gretsch. Billy goes for Mesa Boogie amps and PRS custom guitars, and Eden Bass amps are Paul's favorites.

The band remains very much involved in charities. Most recently Benji and Joel participated in the Challenge for the Children V in Miami Beach, Florida, a weekend devoted to raising money for various children's charities through an *NSYNC-led celebrity basketball game, a skills challenge, and a scavenger hunt. The GC guys remain devoted to jumping at any opportunity that comes their way to help out and make a difference.

Good Charlotte has more than a few tricks up its collective sleeve. Benji and Joel are reportedly set to appear in yet another movie, the John Roecker *Live Freaky! Die Freaky!* "an Epic motion picture of puppet proportions" due out in December 2003 and also featuring Green Day's Billie Joe Armstrong, Fat Mike, and Kelly Osbourne. The band also has plans to start up their own record label with Goldfinger singer John Feldmann. "When you find a band you really like and they're not signed, you think, 'I might actually be able to help them out,' [and] it's cool we can do that," Billy told *MTV News* on February 28, 2003. "Between the label and us wanting to work with other bands, we'll do a bunch of stuff like that." Of course, the twins and Billy have their clothing labels to look after. As for Paul, he's quite happy being the bassist for Good Charlotte at the moment, but when pressed he admits to future aspirations scoring music for movie soundtracks, producing hip-hop, and a possible restaurant joint venture with his sister, a culinary school graduate. Good Charlotte is slated to join in on NOFX's Fat Mike's newest project, a compilation CD entitled *Rock against Bush*. GC will also perform in a show or two during the Rock against Bush tour, designed to convince young music fans to vote against the current president in the next election. Alkaline Trio and Green Day will also be among the bands contributing original songs to the compilation. The tour, which will be a series of free concerts mainly at college campuses, aims to raise political awareness among the eighteen-to-twenty-five-year-old set.

The band is due to start work soon on a third album, slated for a summer 2004 release. They plan to push themselves and to further expand their musical chops, foregoing some hi-tech crutches like ProTools in order to capture a more natural sound—keeping it real, if you like. Fame and fortune haven't impeded Joel and Benji's creative process; they're still writing songs with the same dedication as they did during the late-night sessions in their bedrooms in Waldorf. In fact, they've already got a cauldronful of songs on the backburner, and plan to keep writing throughout the tour. As Joel told *Rolling Stone* on September 3, 2003, "I've been inspired by traveling. We see different countries and lots of different places and meet lots of different people. Traveling around the world opens your mind and puts things in perspective." But don't worry—that signature high-school angst hasn't been exorcised, and the songwriting brothers haven't put the good old days to bed just yet.

Meanwhile, the Young and the Hopeless World Tour is such a triumph that the band has extended dates all the way into the New Year and all the way around the globe, with concerts scheduled in France, the Netherlands, the U.K., and Japan.

Most importantly, the guys of Good Charlotte will keep doing what they love to do: making music. All they ever wanted was to be in a band, and their story is a punk-rock fairy tale come true.

The End.